This book belongs to:

____

____

____

Kojo was a pleasant little boy. He lived with his Mummy, Daddy and his big brother Tim. He loved doing things that were new and exciting. He was not a shy boy and was not easily frightened by things. You could say he was courageous and confident!

When he was a child, Kojo wanted to be a vet. He loved animals and his Mummy encouraged him by bringing home abandoned animals she had rescued.

3

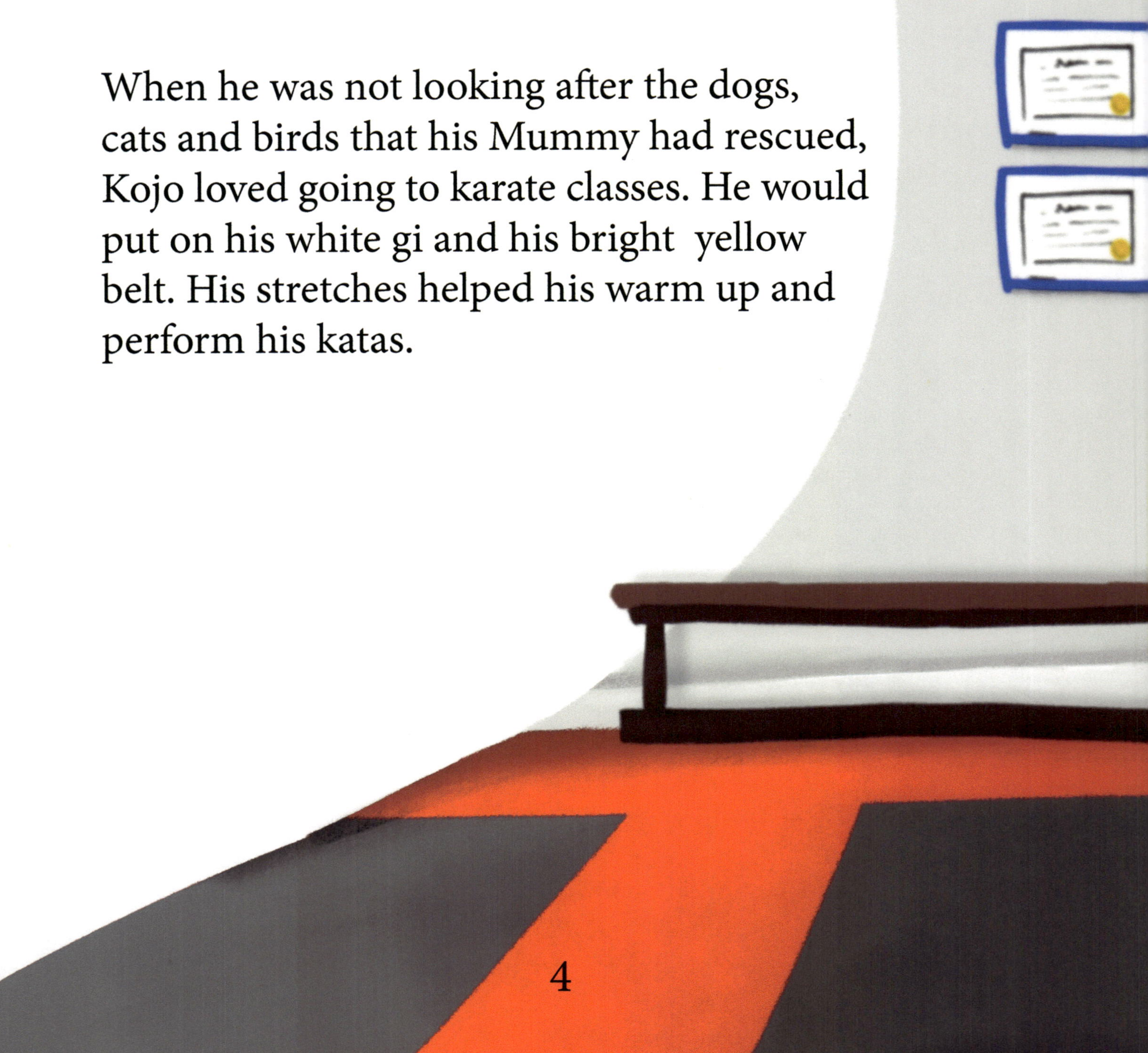

When he was not looking after the dogs, cats and birds that his Mummy had rescued, Kojo loved going to karate classes. He would put on his white gi and his bright yellow belt. His stretches helped his warm up and perform his katas.

4

5

Kojo would go to the local Brownies club, where he and other boys would learn all about how to recognise birds, plants, flowers and stars.

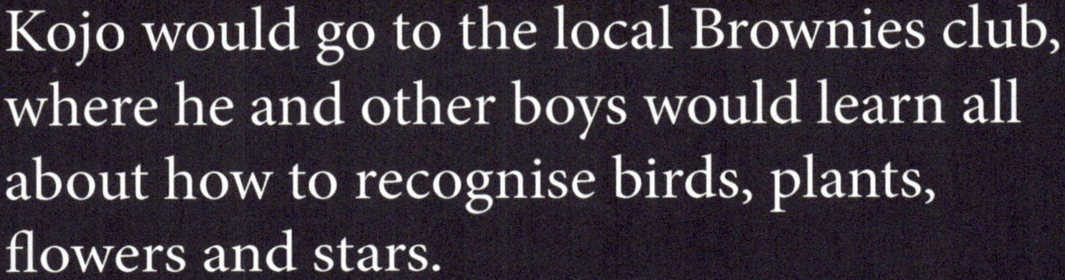

They would also go on camping trips – doing practical things like learning to tie knots and fishing.

He enjoyed sitting around the large camp-fire at night with his friends and their leaders. They would drink hot chocolate and sing songs heartily as the flames quivered and danced.

Kojo's Daddy
was a lorry driver.
He worked shifts
for eight hours each
day and had to drive a
long way for work, taking
important items to lots of
places around Europe.

He often left their home at 2 o'clock
in the morning and drive to the depot
where his lorry was waiting. He would
climb into the cabin and turn on the
engine that growled as its big wheels moved
in synchrony.

Tim and Kojo's Mummy worked as a
meal assistant at their school. She was
always home in the morning and made
them a yummy breakfast to start the
day.

She helped them with their school
lunches and walked home with them
in the afternoon.

Kojo did not mind getting his hands dirty. When there was something important to do. He enjoyed helping his Daddy with light engineering tasks – such as fixing cars for the family and friends in the local town who would call them if their car was broken down.

13

Kojo's Daddy showed him what all of the different
tools were in his garage and how they were used.
Some of them were somewhat heavy and many
were greasy. His Daddy was very clever.

One of the cars they repaired was very
old and various parts were missing. He
managed to fix the car with bits and
pieces and it worked!

Kojo's big brother was very kind
and caring towards his. He helped
his learn to tie his shoelaces and
listened to his reading if Mummy
was too busy cooking dinner in the
kitchen.

After supper, they would walk
their dogs together along the local
high street on the way to the park.
Kojo loved to see all the new small
businesses popping up in the
neighbourhood.

One Autumn, Kojo and Tim wanted to raise money to pay for Christmas presents. They started a car wash business in the street where they lived. They would go from door to door with sponges and buckets. When neighbours opened their doors, Kojo and Tim would smile and offer a good price for making their cars clean and shiny.

It was hard work to do a good job but the neighbours were very happy. They earned quite a lot of money and were able to buy gifts for their parents, cousins and friends.

19

Kojo did well at school, he worked hard, was obedient to his teachers and was liked by the other pupils. When he was in senior school he succeeded in his school examinations.

He applied to university and got a place to study English Literature. He was the first person in his family to go to university and this made them very proud!

21

When his brother Tim
grew older, he began
to travel to other parts of
the world in relation to his
work. He travelled to Africa
and became a micro-farmer in a
country called Burundi.

This meant that he had some
land that was not huge in size
but enabled him and a team of
local people to have a sense of
purpose and grow fruit and
vegetables for their families.

This project was very exciting for Kojo as he was able to travel to see his brother there and made friends with lots of the people in the area. He would take small gifts of pencils, crayons, notebooks and toiletries in his suitcase. The children in the village near the farm would run to see his when he arrived with many large bags of goodies!

NOTEBOOK
NOTEBOOK
25

After three years of hard work, Kojo graduated
from University. He wondered what he should
do next when the opportunity for his to work
as a personal assistant in a bank arose! He did
this with the plan to find a different job that was
linked to his English literature degree later on.

Kojo was very industrious, he worked at the
bank during the day and worked in a restaurant
in the evenings and at weekends. He found the
job in the bank quite interesting because
he realised that banking is about helping
people and this was something he had
always wanted to do.

27

Kojo worked in the Financial Services section of the bank and did a range of junior roles to help small businesses like restaurants, florists, cafés and to get started.

The people he worked with were very nice and they taught his so many aspects of banking and finance. He got better and better at the different tasks and projects.

29

Kojo now has lots of experience and works for a big bank. He works with companies around the world. He has a big team of 85 people working with his and they do wonderful things for lots of people. Some of the people he manages live very far away in Hong Kong and Vietnam.

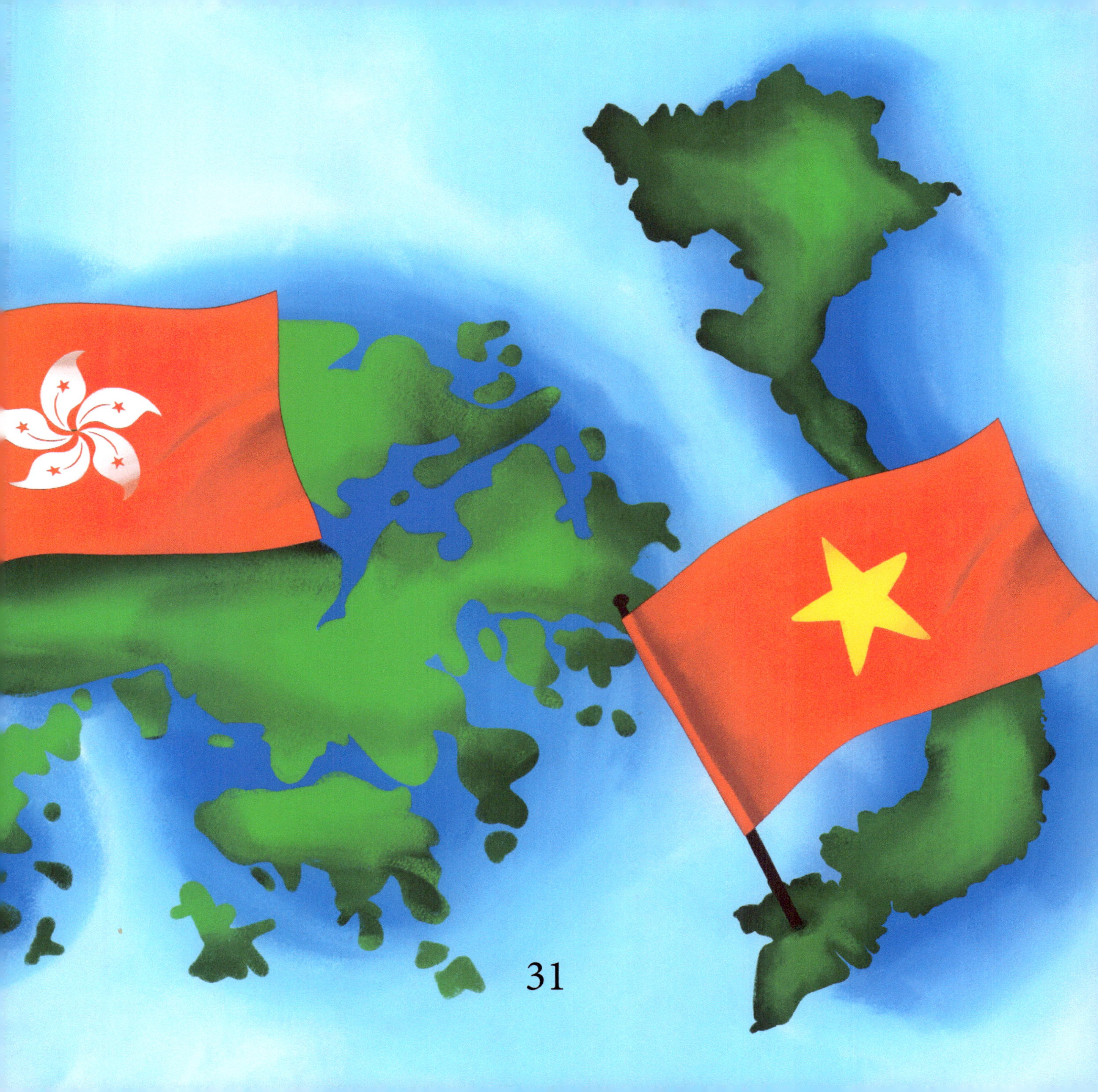

31

As Kojo works with people in other countries, he is now able to speak French, German and Cantonese.

In his spare time, Kojo rescues dogs. The dogs make Kojo feel happy and they can be playful. Being an investment banker and helping businesses to start and flourish is something that Kojo does well.

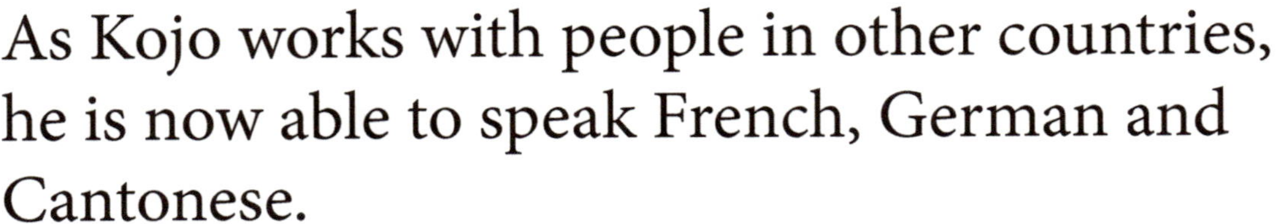

33

Kojo is very passionate about his job where he meets so many entrepreneurs and small business owners who come to his for help. He enjoys teaching them about money and giving them financial advice.

You can be an impressive investment banker, just like Kojo!

BANK

If you want to be an impressive investment banker, take a look at these references to learn how!

For Kids:

NatWest
Practise spotting value for money as you trade with three outlandish alien shopkeepers for a range of space commodities.
https://natwest.mymoneysense.com/students/students-8-12/space-trader/

Cool Kid Facts
Information page for kids on the history of banking and how banks work.
https://www.coolkidfacts.com/how-banks-work/

Ducksters
Information page for kids on economics.
https://www.ducksters.com/money/economics.php

<u>**For parents and guardians:**</u>

The Complete University Guide
Comprehensive UK university league tables for accounting and finance.
https://www.thecompleteuniversityguide.co.uk/league-tables/rankings/accounting-and-finance

Target Careers
Information on how to begin a career in finance.
https://targetcareers.co.uk/career-sectors/finance/70-how-do-i-get-into-finance

Indeed.com
Advice page on career paths within banking.
https://www.indeed.com/career-advice/career-development/career-paths-banking

What do you want to be when you grow up? Draw it below!

Notes!

....

....

....

....

....

....

....

....

....

....

....

....

Check out some other books in the series!

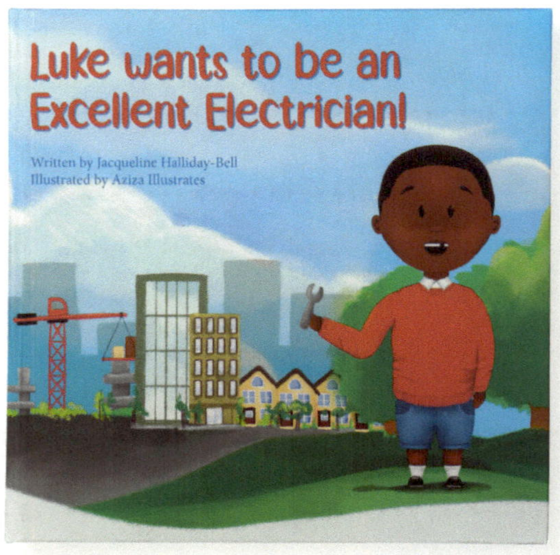